PETALS OF LIGHT
Christmas Blessings

ADRIANA VOLONA

Title:	*Petals of Light - Christmas Blessings*
Author:	Adriana Volona
ISBN:	ISBN: 978-1-7641936-2-7
Copyright	© October 2025 All rights are reserved. No part of this book is to be reproduced or transmitted without written permission from the author.
Published by:	Volona Books
Contributor:	Paula Volona - Layout and Design With special acknowledgment to Adobe Firefly for AI generated images used as part of the creative process in the composition of artwork in this book.

This book is dedicated to
"all people of goodwill"

Preface

Petals of Light - Christmas Blessings is a reflective piece which explores a wide range of meanings associated with Christmas. The birth of Jesus Christ is experienced as a major blessing for the whole of humanity, regardless of race or religion. As the Christmas Angel proclaimed: *'Peace to all of good will on earth'*.

The themes of love associated with the coming and message of Jesus Christ are about: harmonious communities, nurturing, repairing broken relationships, treasuring bonds of connection, forgiveness, equality and justice, compassion, gratitude, joy, and inclusiveness.

Each large alphabetical character in this book represents a Christmas theme and blessing for a better world where all the living co-exist in peace. Flowers are also depicted because they are historically gifted in most traditions as a symbol of love.

These large alphabetical characters are sequenced together to bring a Christmas message of blessing to the reader. This message is found on the last page.

Adriana Volona

... is for the blessing of

HOPE

Christmas is about consciously hoping for a better future for everyone in the world in the upcoming New Year.

... is for the blessing of

AFFIRMATION and ACKNOWLEDGMENT

Christmas is about acknowledging and affirming each others' strengths and special qualities that inspire and nurture us in our lives.

... is for the blessing of
PEACE-MAKING

Christmas is about
making a special effort
to bring peace of mind and heart
to others and ourselves.

... is for the blessing of
PATIENCE
Christmas is about consciously being patient and forgiving with ourselves and with each other's shortcomings.

... is for the blessing of
YEARNING
Christmas is about consciously yearning for an end to the suffering of all the living - human, animal and environmental.

... is for the blessing of
COMPASSION
Christmas is about consciously sending compassion to all the living, especially to bring relief to those suffering physically, emotionally, mentally and spiritually.

... is for the blessing of

HEALING

Christmas is about
helping the healing
of what has been wounded.

... is for the blessing of
RECONCILIATION
and
RESTORATION

Christmas is about consciously seeking to reconcile and restore broken relationships.

... is for the blessing of
INCLUSIVENESS
Christmas is about
being consciously inclusive
of those isolated, excluded
and marginalized.

... is for the blessing of
SHARING
Christmas is about consciously sharing our resources with those who lack them.

... is for the blessing of
THANKSGIVING
Christmas is about being consciously thankful for all the blessings we have received.

... is for the blessing of

MESSAGES OF LOVE

Christmas is about
consciously sending
genuine messages of love
to those in our lives
with whom we are in contact.

... is for the blessing of

ATTUNEMENT

Christmas is about consciously
attuning to who we are and
what our purpose is
for being on this planet.

... is for the blessing of
SINGING
Christmas is about singing
the joy we feel in the harmony
created by our togetherness.

... is for the blessing of
WELLNESS

Christmas is about wishing wellness towards everyone, including those we resent and disapprove.

... is for the blessing of
INSPIRATION
Christmas is about inspiring one another to believe in the best within us all.

... is for the blessing of

SUPPORT

Christmas is about offering support to those we discover need it, and being grateful for the support we have received throughout the year.

... is for the blessing of

HARMONY

Christmas is about creating and celebrating harmony amongst us all.

... is for the blessing of
INSIGHT
Christmas is about reflecting on the insights of Jesus Christ, whose birth and life is the focus of this celebration.

... is for the blessing of
NURTURING
Christmas is a time of special nurturing of one another by spending time together and sharing a special meal with each other.

... is for the blessing of
GIFT-GIVING
Christmas is a time of gift-giving to others, especially children, as a way of showing our appreciation for their presence in our lives.

... is for the blessing of

YOUTH

Christmas is a time we show how much we value children and youth – their joyful exuberance, innocence and excitement lift our spirits.

... is for the blessing of
OPEN-HEARTEDNESS
Christmas is a time of remembering to be open-hearted in our attitude towards others and ourselves.

... is for the blessing of

UNIVERSALITY

Christmas brings a universal message that everyone in the world is equally important and valuable, beyond religion, race, culture, economic and social status.

... is for the blessing of
INCARNATION
Christmas is about
the incarnation of Love
in human form.

... is for the blessing of
NOURISHMENT

Christmas is a time
we specifically focus
on nourishing our
souls, minds, hearts
and bodies.

... is for the blessing of
NEARNESS
Christmas is about remembering
the nearness of God in our lives -
we are not alone.

... is for the blessing of
ENTHUSIASM
Christmas is about
an enthusiasm for new life
and new beginnings.

... is for the blessing of
RENEWAL
Christmas is about
renewing our commitment
to care for one another
to the best of our ability.

P

... is for the blessing of

PROVIDENCE

Christmas is about celebrating the providence of God in Jesus Christ.

... is for the blessing of
EMBRACING
Christmas is a special time
of embracing one another
both near and far.

... is for the blessing of
ACTIVITY
Christmas is a time
when there is lots of activity
in preparation for the
special celebration.

... is for the blessing of

CELEBRATION
and CONNECTION

Christmas is a time
of celebrating and connecting
with everyone we love.

... is for the blessing of

ECUMENISM

Christmas is celebrated ceremonially and ecumenically across more than 45,000 Christian denominations, and more broadly amongst non-Christians as a seasonal holiday.

HAPPY CHRISTMAS

WISHING YOU INNER PEACE

www.ingramcontent.com/pod-product-compliance
Lightning Source LLC
LaVergne TN
LVHW010019070426
835507LV00001B/2